Domestic violence
essence, meaning, support

by

Valentin Boyadzhiev
member of ISAP, IAHT, АБПП

Contents

Introduction

Dear ladies and gentlemen, it is my pleasure to present you the book **"Domestic violence - essence, meaning, support"**. The book consists of 9 topics in which we will examine in detail the problem related to Domestic violence. The topic is important for society and the individual. Knowledge of the problem and methods of dealing with it is crucial for any person and specialist who has contact with people in a similar state. I hope that this book will bring some light to the issues and enrich your knowledge and experience and help you or your loved ones to deal with this problem!

In this book, you will learn what is violence and how exactly is manifested, which factors strengthen the trend toward violence. What is domestic violence and when your partner is prone to it? What are the types of domestic violence? Why it is very important to talk about this problem and what can be the misconceptions about it? How can we help a person who is a victim of domestic violence? How can you help yourself in case of that kind of violence? What are the natural reactions of victims of domestic violence? Consequences of violence against women and what are the signs of identification of the victim of violence.

This book is suitable for: Psychologists, Psychiatrists, Teachers, Pedagogues, Social Workers, Medical Practitioners, Nurses, Parents, Academicians, Students, Parents, Families, Partners and Anyone Interested In the topic of Domestic Violence.

About the author

Valentin Boyadzhiev is a trained nutritionist, graduated Master of Psychology in "Psychology and Psychopathology of Development". He has acquired Professional Qualification "Teacher of Psychology" and Postgraduate Professional Qualification "Psychological Counseling in Psychosomatic and Social Adaptation Disorders". He has obtained a Psychoanalysis Diploma and he has specialized in Psychoanalytic Psychotherapy. He is a member of the Association "Bulgarian Psychoanalytic Space", "International Society of Applied Psychoanalysis" and „International Alliance of Holistic Therapists". He is a lecturer on issues related to nutrition, diet, supplementation, food, and sports. He is also a teacher and a lecturer in the field of psychology, logic, ethics, law, and philosophy. He has been a school psychologist since 2017. He has been participating annually in scientific conferences on psychology, psychotherapy, dietetics, and medicine. His main interest and practice are in the field of psychoanalysis and clinical psychology.

What is violence?

Violence - "Any act or behaviour directed against the other person or self that causes physical, mental or emotional suffering can be called violence. By its social nature, violence is an anti-human act."

Violence is manifested in various obvious and non-obvious forms (like pedagogical violence, information violence, manipulative violence, indifferent violence, etc.). There is both physical and mental violence (for example imposing restrictions, controlling, isolating, depreciating and underestimating, manipulation through children, making the partner economically dependent), there are also various causes at the macro-level (like lack of values, lack of positive models) and at the personal level (e.g. deficits in socialization and realization, distrust in others, loss of consciousness for justice, the low threshold of inhibitions in aggression, lack of strategy for conflict resolution) and all of these play an important role in the behaviour.

Various environmental factors strengthen the trend toward violence.

These are factors such as:
- **The socio-economic crisis and its consequences** - a factor that threatens the physical survival of individuals or families and causes spiritual discouragement;
- **The Mass media** - a factor that threatens the construction of the adolescent value system and, in a sense, provokes the use of violence

as a mechanism for conflict resolution;

- **Globalization** - a factor that threatens the self-realization of the individual. In a global society, one is aware of his imperfection and is more often depressed.
- **Alienation** - a factor that threatens community togetherness as a group and provokes mistrust and insecurity;
- **Social devaluation** - a factor that threatens the preservation of spiritual identity. The lack of values and orientation is reflected mainly regressive of the human race.

WHAT IS DOMESTIC VIOLENCE?

If you have ever been hit, physically injured, or threatened with injury by your partner when he or she was angry, you have been a victim of domestic violence. Even threats not related to physical violence are a sign of a problem.

If your partner breaks or throws objects when angry, then he/she is aggressive towards you.

If you are often offended or yelled at, you are a victim of verbal abuse.

Ask yourself if you are afraid to go home because you may be injured. If yes, you have a problem.

Consider if your friend or partner does some of the following things:

- Yelling, insulting, humiliating, or hitting you;
- Treats you like an item belonging to him/her;
- Constantly controls you, commands you, makes all decisions individually, does not comply with you and is not interested in your opinion;
- Abuses you, easily loses control, boasts that he/she behaves badly with others too;
- Imposes sexual relations against your desire and threatens you;
- Tries to manipulate you, to blackmail you, i.e. saying things like "If you really love me, you will ... "
- Uses drugs and alcohol and induce you to use them;

- Considers that you must always back down and be "obedient".

If even one of those things is happening to you, it can be violence.

Your partner is prone to violence if:
- he/she is almost always aggressive;
- he/she is aggressive towards pets;
- there are criminal episodes in his/her past;
- he/she is subject to a rapid change of mood - from calm to rage;
- he/she blames you for any problems;
- he/she threatens to commit suicide if you leave;
- he/she is always angry at someone or something, breaking and throwing things.

TYPES OF DOMESTIC VIOLENCE

Physical violence is present when:
- You are being pushed;
- He/she strikes, kicks, slaps you;
- Throws objects;
- Threatens or injures you with a weapon;
- Physically impedes your attempt to leave your home;
- He/she locks you somewhere;
- Refuses to help you when you are sick, injured, pregnant;
- Prevents you from seeking medical help;
- Beat the children;
- Threatens your relatives and friends with physical violence;

Sexual abuse can be if:

- He/she forces you to undress against your will;
- Or forces you to have sexual intercourse against your will;
- Or when he/she forces you to have sexual intercourse after a beating;
- Performs sexual intercourse with extreme cruelty;
- Deliberately deprives you of sexual contact;
- Shows extreme jealousy and accuses you of loving relationships with anyone;
- Forces you to watch and/or repeat pornographic acts;

Emotional abuse occurs when:

- He/she constantly criticizes you, screams and/or insults you (for example, tells you that you are too fat or too skinny, that you are stupid and dull, that you are a bad mother, wife, lover);

- Or when your partner ignores your feelings;
- Makes fun of your beliefs;
- Forbids you to go to work;
- Manipulates you by using a lie;
- Offends your relatives and friends in order to remove them from your life;
- Refuses to go out with you and meet other people;
- Prevents you from maintaining relationships with your relatives and friends;
- Does not allow you to make phone calls;
- Completely controls the family budget and makes financial decisions on its own;

- Misappropriate all family income, does not give at all or does not give enough money for the household; he himself does not shop but accuses you of not caring for the family;
- Humiliates you in front of people;
- Threatens to leave or evicts you from home;
- Threatens to take your children;
- Systematically and unjustly punishes the children or do not let you near them;

WHY DOMESTIC VIOLENCE SHOULD NOT BE LEFT UNSAID?

There are several recurring scenarios where victims try to convince themselves that they have not been the victim of violence:

- You think he/she's too sweet to be a bully. And he/she probably is when doesn't hurt you, but that doesn't mean you weren't hurt. Some seem so nice to other people when they are in a good mood or when they hide their anger, but when they lose patience, they tend to be cruel.

- You think it's your fault. This is very common. People usually blame the victim for the violence she is subjected to. For example, someone might say, "What did you do that caused him/her to throw a bottle at you?" The answer to this question is nothing wrong. Victims are not the cause of violence!

- You think that if you are not physically injured, then you are not a victim of violence. When your partner throws a bottle in the room and it doesn't hit you, you believe that he just threw the bottle without wanting to hurt you. In fact, if he/she starts throwing or breaking, it's domestic violence.

- Even a single case of physical violence or threat of physical abuse could be sufficient to establish control over the partner. This power could then be consolidated through controlling behaviours that exclude physical violence. For example, a verbal attack after physical bullying carries the additional threat that new physical abuse may ensue. In this way, oral threats are sufficient to allow the abuser to consolidate his control without actually hurting the victim's body.

- You tell yourself that he/she will change and get better. This happens when you realize that you are a victim of domestic violence, but consider it a single case. It is very dangerous to think that way. If someone dares to hurt you once, they will repeat it (this can happen in days, weeks, or months). The question is not whether this will happen again, but when. The only way to end the vicious practice is to seek qualified help.

First of all, understand that your tormentor is ultimately weak, not strong. And if you tolerate his humiliation tacitly and obediently, your patience can further irritate him and strengthen his sense that everything is allowed. Therefore, silence is not the best tactic of behaviour. But both the cries and the tears are a poor demonstration of your suffering and also increase the activity of the abuser. First of all, if the situation has not gone too far, resist violence, not physically but morally. If violence in your family has existed for a long time and the abuser is already accustomed to your obedience, resistance can only provoke him to take more decisive action - it may even lead to a murder caused by the fear that his "object" has stood against him. In such a situation, first of all, realize what exactly made you live such a long time with a person who has been committing an atrocity with you all the time. It's time to think about how to break away from your abuser. And even if you are financially dependent on him/her - decide what you would like more: being financially secure but humiliated, or being an independent and strong person.

HOW CAN WE HELP A PERSON WHO IS A VICTIM OF DOMESTIC VIOLENCE?

1. We can try to understand him/her well:

- To listen, not to condemn the victim and show that we're on her/his side.
- To show that we consider her/his feelings reasonable and normal.
- To give the victim time to make own decisions without advising to return to the partner abuser trying to repair their relationship. Let's not push to make quick decisions.
- Let the victim talk about the emotional side of this relationship and not criticize for living with this

abusive partner. Let's try to explain that, if no action is taken, the couple's violence will progress.

- Help the victim emphasize the positive in what's happening. We should not tell that he/she is obliged to stand with the partner abuser for the sake of the children, on the contrary.

- We should congratulate her/him for finding the strength and courage to speak. That shows that the victim feels her/his family is both harmful and inappropriate for both own mental health and the normal growth of the children. The fact that the victim shares mean that she/he is taking the first steps to secure a better life for herself/himself and the children.

- We must respect her/his need to keep a secret if we are asked to.

2. We can try to help the victim connect with services that support people who have experienced violence:

- Find out what support organizations for victims of violence are available in the city or region. Tell the victim about them. Consider the needs of the individual and find out if organizations also can take care of the children, if there are any.
- If you are trying to help in a situation of psychological or physical abuse, persuade the victim to seek help from the police.

3. What could we say to the victim?

- Express clear and concise messages such as: "Violence is always unacceptable." "There is never a valid excuse for it."

- The safety of women and children is paramount.
- The victim is not the cause of violence. Responsible for that is solely the partner abuser.
- The victim will not be able to change either the abuser or his behaviour.
- Apologies and big promises will not end the violence.
- The victim is not alone with this problem.
- Violence is not a loss of control. This is the behaviour that people use to control others.
- Violence has traumatic consequences for children.
- Under the Domestic and Family Violence Protection Act, beating your partner is a crime. Protection under this law may be sought by any person who has suffered domestic

violence perpetrated by a spouse or ex-spouse; a partner with whom they live together under the same roof and with a common budget; a partner with a child etc.

- You can try to convince the victim that she/he should seek help from police and organizations that support victims of violence.

The victim may be frightened and confused and unable to act quick and efficient to take action. However, the very fact that the victim is trying to seek help and assistance is encouraging. Each time efforts are made in this direction, she/he becomes more confident in making bolder decisions.

SAFETY PLAN

Thoroughly consider your actions in the face of the risk of re-violence, prepare a safety plan and prepare for its implementation.

Call the police immediately if there is an emergency. If you are unable to do so, your neighbours can do it for you.

Make arrangements with your neighbours to call the police if they hear screams from your house or apartment.

Learn the local phone numbers that can provide you with the support you need (crisis centre for women, helpline, etc.).

Tell about the violence of those you trust (friends, relatives).

Prepare yourself a place to go in case of danger.

If you cannot avoid a dispute or an incident, try to choose an appropriate room for disputing that can easily be escaped from if necessary. Try to avoid disputes in rooms that do not have access to outside doors (such as the bathroom or kitchen where there are sharp and cutting objects).

Consider leaving your home quickly and safely. Determine which doors, windows, stairs are best suited for this.

Beforehand, leave with your friends or relatives spare clothes, important documents, phone numbers, required medications, and more.

Try to destroy all the possible ways that could help your abuser find you (notebooks, diaries, envelopes with addresses, etc.).

If the situation is critical, leave your home immediately, even if you have not been able to bring the necessary things with you. Remember that your life is in danger!

When leaving your home, do your best to bring your children with you.

If you are beaten or abused, get a medical certificate immediately.

WHAT ARE THE NATURAL REACTIONS OF VICTIMS OF DOMESTIC VIOLENCE?

In assessing the victim's condition, consideration should be given to the intensity of mental trauma. When the victim is in a state of traumatic or post-traumatic stress, it may be possible to observe behaviour that may seem at first glance illogical and disturbing. These reactions are normal reactions to an abnormal event in human life.

The severity of the symptomatology depends on factors such as:

- age;

- a physical and mental condition of the victim;
- previous experience with similar situations;
- the adequate response of the police officer;
- support from the family, professional and social community.

Some of the symptoms and normal reactions of the victim of domestic violence could be one or more of the following:

1. Fear
- from death or physical injury to yourself or someone you love;
- of being left alone;
- of "loss of control" over yourself;
- that such events can be repeated.

2. Helplessness

- The event triggers your powerlessness or helplessness.

3. Sadness

- for fear of death, injuries and other grievous losses.

4. Sorrow

- because of what happened

5. Guilt

- because of what you had to experience;
- regret what you did not do or what you could have done earlier;

6. Shame

- because you have shown yourself to be helpless and in need of help from others;

- because you did not react as you would wish to react and did not do what you should.

7. Anger

- to what has happened and to the person who is the cause of what has happened;
- to the injustice of everything that happens;
- because of the shame and insult experienced;
- because of a lack of understanding from other people and because of unsuccessful attempts to explain their condition to them.

8. Recalling

- feelings related to the presence of the abuser in your life

9. Disappointment

- by yourself, by people or life.

10. Hope

- for the future, for better times.

11. Physical feelings and mental states

- You may also have physical sensations that may or may not be related to the feelings described. Sometimes they occur many months after a crisis. Some common sensations are fatigue, insomnia, nightmares, vague anxiety, vague thoughts, memory and concentration impairment, dizziness, palpitations, trembling, difficulty breathing, suffocation, throat heaviness, muscle tension that can lead to a headache.

12. Social relations

- Tensions may arise with your relatives. Good relationships with children can turn into conflicts. You may feel that even minor things are out of balance, you cannot react the way your loved ones expect you to, and you feel that communication requires too much.

An acute stress reaction occurs immediately at the time of the stressful event and is associated with:
- the initial state of numbness;
- narrowing of attention and disorientation;
- withdrawal from the stressful situation;
- depression;
- excessive anxiety, self-isolation;
- agitation, anger, hyperactivity.

Partial or complete amnesia may be observed during the traumatic event. In such cases, it is advisable to remove the victim quickly from a stressful situation. Usually, the symptoms quickly go away and the victim can be treated painlessly. If this does not happen, the symptoms start to disappear spontaneously after 24-48 hours to 3 days.

Post-traumatic stress disorder occurs when the traumatic response is not well managed and the victim is unable to cope with the trauma. This is a delayed response to a stressful event. The symptoms of Posttraumatic stress disorder (PTSD) are:

- episodes of repetitive experience of the trauma as a sudden recollection of individual fragments of the situation;

- experiences in the form of dreams, nightmares;
- a continuing feeling of numbness and emotional dullness;
- hostility to others;
- mood loss, appetite, sleep disorders;
- Avoiding actions and signals that are reminiscent of a traumatic situation.

Reactions of the victim of the crime other than traumatic and posttraumatic stress:

- Feelings of guilt and self-blame. These symptoms are common in sexual offences and domestic violence. Often, this feeling is instilled by the abuser in order to provide with "silence" from the victim.
- Feelings of helplessness and fear. Generating fear and anxiety, as effects of violence, can lead to

negative changes in the victim's social behaviour and thus the sense of security can be hurt.

- Paradoxical reactions such as laughter or devaluation of what happened.
- Uncontrollable anger and aggression and redirection of angry reactions to neutral subjects, mainly to law enforcement representatives. This is a common reaction and is paradoxical in domestic violence. However, such behaviour is not an expression of a personal attitude towards the law and order officer. The victim needs immediate relief and anger is an intense emotional state. The object of this anger is the abuser, but not always the victim-perpetrator relationship allows the adequate release of the emotion, in

which case the anger is diverted to a more accessible object.

What the victim of violence is experiencing?

The systemic and incidental experience of violence leads to a change in personality. The experience of violence affects the quality of coping with everyday tasks. It causes negative mental states that violate the established dynamic stereotype. The experience of violence is seen as an event that triggers a crisis of existence. The consequences of experiencing violence can be described as posttraumatic stress disorder. It can be detected in the victim's behaviour and his/her state of health. The abused, humiliated, injured, a raped person lives in fear. Fear changes the victim's self-esteem. **Fear provokes:**

- low self-esteem and depreciation of life;
- feeling self-hatred;
- meeting the requirements of the abuser;
- rejection of one's own opinion;
- compromise with one's own principles and needs;
- feelings of guilt and helplessness;
- misuse of various substances;
- chronic anxiety;
- membership in different groups.

The victim is dissatisfied with the interpersonal interaction and the life perspective is meaningless. Life without a compass is a prerequisite for self-isolation, aggression or self-aggression.

Consequences of violence against women

Silence:

- Violence becomes a taboo topic. Women who are victims of violence make every effort to conceal it. The pain and humiliation experienced only lives in the mind of the woman.

The reasons may be:

- Imposing a sense of guilt in the victim.
- Recognizing own weakness first to oneself and then in the outside world.

The result usually could be:

- Unlocking mental illness.
- The victim becomes an abuser.
- Building a victim identity.

The usual **internal contradiction** is caused, on the one hand, by the woman's desire to "forget" about the violence, to erase it from her consciousness and to continue to live as if it had never happened. On the other hand, stays the need to speak about it and thus begin to part with the difficult memories.

Guilt:

- The generally accepted norm that the victim is guilty is experienced as a personal conviction. The woman who has been the victim of violence lives with the thought that she causes it. She believes that if she changes and becomes better, the violence will stop.

Loss of self-belief:

- The woman feels helpless and passive, unable to cope alone with the situation. It also determines her low self-esteem. The victim is "crushed" mentally, feeling humiliated, unworthy, defective.

State of dependency:

- Women victims of violence find themselves in a situation where they can anticipate violence but cannot escape it. Strong emotional, family or financial dependence causes the woman to stay with the abuser.

Contradictory feelings:

- Often the woman victim of violence still loves her partner, but this love is accompanied by fear for physical and mental survival. This state of intense confusion makes her indecisive.

Change in interpersonal relationships:

- There is a lack of trust in relationships between people, which is often expressed in beliefs such as: "All men are equal"; "Even if I find another man, he will be the same as the previous one"; "No one can help me."

Suicidal thoughts and suicide attempts:

- The desperation and hopelessness of the situation prompt some women to end their lives.

The crisis:

- The emotional state in which a woman falls after an act of violence is often described as a crisis. In such a state, emotions are very intense, fears are heightened and the woman is confused.

Remember, you can always find someone to help you. Therefore, when you are a victim of domestic violence, we ask that you seek the assistance of the police and the specialized organizations that assist the victims of violence.

Signs of identification of the victim of violence

Children:

- introversy,
- apathy,
- aggressive behaviour,
- strong crying,
- emotional dependence,
- avoidance of visual contact,
- indiscriminate attachment.

In sexual abuse:

- sexual behaviour,
- rigidity,
- emotional dependence,
- passiveness,
- introversy,
- overexcitement,
- difficulty in eating.

Adolescence:
- introversy,
- apathy,
- aggressive and self-destructive behaviour,
- self-harm,
- problems at school,
- fear of failure,
- misuse of various substances,
- escape from home.

In sexual abuse:
- sexual behaviour,
- inability to attach to adolescents of the same age,
- distraction,
- eating disorders like bulimia, anorexia, obesity,
- problems at school.

Youth:
- introversy,

- apathy,
- aggressive and antisocial behaviour,
- misunderstanding with young people of the same age and seeking adult attention,
- running away from home and drinking,
- taking drugs, etc.,
- problems at school.

In sexual abuse:

- sexual behaviour and posturing,
- debauchery and prostitution,
- disobedience or kindliness, leading to extreme isolation,
- fear,
- self-harm,
- symptoms of suicide,
- pseudo-maturity,
- eating disorders,
- alcohol and drug abuse.

Adults:

- an inability to maintain long-lasting and satisfying relationships,
- poor self-esteem,
- fear,
- anger and situations of violence.

In the case of sexual abuse:

- sexual problems,
- distrust,
- a shame of the body,
- inability to assert oneself,
- feeling victimized,
- abuse of alcohol or drugs,
- poor self-esteem.

Final Words

Thanks to everyone who was interested in this book. I hope each of you has been able to bring out the knowledge he needs so that he can help both himself and the people he loves.

www.ingramcontent.com/pod-product-compliance
Lightning Source LLC
Chambersburg PA
CBHW051125250726
48655CB00007B/2885